100 facts
Plant Life

Camilla de la Bedoyere

Consultant: Barbara Taylor

Miles KeLLy

First published in 2012 by Miles Kelly Publishing Ltd
Harding's Barn, Bardfield End Green, Thaxted, Essex, CM6 3PX, UK

Copyright © Miles Kelly Publishing Ltd 2012

1 2 3 4 5 6 7 8 9 10

Publishing Director Belinda Gallagher
Creative Director Jo Cowan
Editorial Director Rosie McGuire
Senior Editor Carly Blake
Volume Designers Andrea Slane,
 Simon Lee, Kayleigh Allen
Cover Designer Kayleigh Allen
Image Manager Liberty Newton
Indexer Gill Lee
Production Manager Elizabeth Collins
Reprographics Stephan Davis,
 Anthony Cambray, Jennifer Hunt,
 Thom Allaway

ISBN 978-1-84810-615-4

Printed in China

British Library Cataloguing-in-Publication Data
A catalogue record for this book is available from the British Library

BGCI is a global network of botanic
gardens working together to prevent
the extinction of plant species.
Making sure that plants are
conserved will help to ensure a
sustainable future for our planet.
www.bgci.org

BGCI
Plants for the Planet

The publishers would like to thank Botanic Gardens
Conservation International for their help in compiling this book.

ACKNOWLEDGEMENTS

The publishers would like to thank the following artists
who have contributed to this book:
Ian Jackson, Stuart Jackson-Carter, Mike Foster at Maltings Partnership
All other artwork from the Miles Kelly Artwork Bank

The publishers would like to thank the following sources for the
use of their photographs:
t = top, b = bottom, l = left, r = right, c = centre, bg = background
Cover Front: Elan Sun Star/Corbis Back: Beboy/Shutterstock.com
Alamy 7(tl) Derek Harris; 18(b) Science Photo Library;
28(b) Stephen Frink Collection
Corbis 26(bl) Wayne Lynch/All Canada Photos; 30(c) David Ponton/
Design Pics; 36 Martin Harvey
Dreamstime 7(tr) Surz01; 25(persimmon) Carla720, (ragwort) Rmorijn;
30(br) Egonzitter; 33(rubber tree) Braendan, (tyre) Chuyu
FLPA 19(br) Wayne Hutchinson; 26(tr) Hiroya Minakuchi/Minden Pictures;
27(tr) Grant Dixon/Minden Pictures, (c) Tim Fitzharris/Minden Pictures;
33 Konrad Wothe/Imagebroker
Fotolia.com 2(paper) pdtnc; 11(round leaf) AndreyTTL; 30(butterfly) Dmytro
Fomin, (squirrel) Dave Timms; 33(banana) Darren Hester, (cocoa pod) Shariff
Che'Lah, (chocolate) Maksim Shebeko
Getty 32(c) Visuals Unlimited, Inc./Thomas Marent
iStockphoto.com 4(bl), 5(tr) spxChrome; 15(cr) Sergey Chushkin,
(titan arum) Tim Messick; 20(b) JPhilipson, (l) Ruud de Man;
25(horse chestnut) Marko Roeper; 30(badger) Chris Crafter; 34(t) Terraxplorer
National Geographic Stock 28(br) James P. Blair
Naturepl.com 16 Solvin Zankl; 18–19 Jurgen Freund; 18(cl) Neil Lucas;
28 Tim Fitzharris/Minden Pictures
NHPA 21(tr) Anthony Bannister
Photolibrary UK 13(t); 17(tr); 22 Ed Reschke; 25(r) Natalie Tepper
Rex Features 39(tr) KPA/Zuma, (c) Dean Houlding
Science Photo Library 6(cl) Martin Shields; 15(cl) Bjorn Rorslett;
16(c) Susumu Nishinaga; 20(r) Power and Syred; 37(b) Simon Fraser
Shutterstock.com 1 PhotoLiz; 2(bamboo frame) Scorpp; 3(b) Tungphoto;
4(tl) Iurii Konoval; 5(br) PhotoHappiness; 6–7(bg) Scapinachis; 6(t) Terric
Delayn, (b) WendellandCarolyn, (mud) Ultrashock, (lined paper) Katrina Brown;
7(yellow paper) Kanate; 8–9(bg) Pablo H Caridad; 8(tr) Imageman;
9(tl) Dr. Morley Read, (c) Vaclav Volrab, (cr) Anna Kucherova, (br) Sergii
Figurnyi; 10(bl) Valentina_G, (paper) Happydancing; 11(oval and long leaves)
Maxstockphoto, (compound leaf) SlavaK, (needle) Oleksandr Kostiuchenko,
(b) Ron Rowan Photography; 12(tl) Ales Liska; 13(bl) Irin-k; 14–15(bg)
T. Kimmeskamp; 15(bird of paradise flower) Steve Heap, (bee orchid)
Witchcraft; 19(t) Richard A. McGuirk; 20(bl) Konstanttin; 21(c) Clinton Moffat;
23(t) Cathy Keifer; 25(border) Nyasha, (stinging nettle) Marilyn Barbone,
(thorns) Mexrix; 26–27(bg) AlessandroZocc; 26(tl) Ronstik, (bl) Hank Frentz,
(stamp) AlexanderZam; 27(tl) Irena Misevic; 28(cl) Shi Yali; 30–31(globes)
Anton Balazh; 30 Inga Nielsen, (bluejay) Mike Truchon, (chipmunk and fox)
Eric Isselée, (hedgehog) Ok.nazarenko, (mole) Tramper, (owl) Tomatto, (worm)
Dusty Cline; 31(tr) Natalia Bratslavsky; 32(bg) Szefei; 33(r) Quang Ho,
(banana flower) Tungphoto, (coffee berries) Matuchaki, (vanilla pods) LianeM;
34(cl) Elena Schweitzer, (b) Alaettin YILDIRIM, (bl) Mark Winfrey;
35(r) Erperlstrom, (echinacea) Elena Elisseeva, (pomegranate) Viktar
Malyshchyts, (willow bark) Marilyn Barbone, (ginseng) Sunsetman;
37(cr) 3355m, (paper) Stephen Aaron Rees; 38–39(bg) Tania Zbrodko;
38(r) Urosr

All other photographs are from:
Corel, digitalSTOCK, digitalvision, John Foxx, PhotoAlto, PhotoDisc,
PhotoEssentials, PhotoPro, Stockbyte

Every effort has been made to acknowledge the source and
copyright holder of each picture.
Miles Kelly Publishing apologises for any unintentional errors or omissions.

Made with paper from a sustainable forest

www.mileskelly.net
info@mileskelly.net
www.factsforprojects.com

CONTENTS

Our green planet

1 Our planet is the only place in the known Universe where plants can grow. It is thanks to these living things that we have air to breathe and food to eat. They make the Earth an exciting, dynamic home to an enormous variety of animals and billions of people.

2 Most plants have leaves, stems, roots and flowers. However, there are many exceptions, such as cacti, pine trees, ferns, and cushions of moss that grow on rocks. No one knows exactly how many different species (types) of plants there are, but the number is thought to be around 450,000. Scientists are discovering new species every day.

3 The first plants to grow on land appeared more than 500 million years ago. That's more than three billion years after the first signs of life on Earth. Today, plants survive in many different environments, from the icy Arctic to hot, dry deserts and steamy tropical forests.

▼ A forest is much more than just a collection of trees. It is home to millions of plants and animals, as well as people.

What is a plant?

4 Plants are living things that, like animals, are able to do seven important things. They can move, grow, breathe, feed, reproduce (make new plants), make waste products and react to their surroundings.

5 While animals have to find food, plants are able to make their own. They use energy from sunlight to turn carbon dioxide and water into a sugary food. This process is called photosynthesis (say: foto-sin-the-sis) (see page 10).

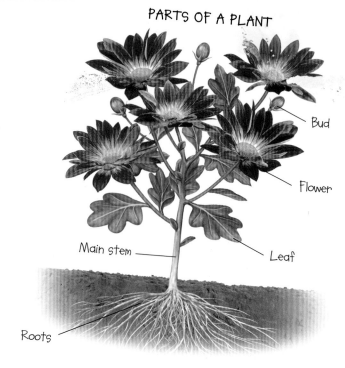

PARTS OF A PLANT

Bud

Flower

Main stem

Leaf

Roots

▲ Most plants have the same basic form, with roots, stems and leaves. Some plants, known as angiosperms, also grow flowers.

▼ The oval leaflets on a mimosa plant move and fold inwards when they are touched.

6 Plants are able to find out about their environment, and react to it. Animals use eyes, ears and other organs to sense their surroundings, but the way plants do this is much simpler. Their roots can sense water in the soil, and their leaves move towards sunlight when they detect it.

▼ Here, squash seedlings grow towards light to receive as much energy as possible.

FAST GROWING
Bamboo – up to
30 centimetres per day

◄ Bamboo is a type of grass, and one of the fastest-growing plants on the planet.

7 In the right circumstances, some plants never stop growing. Bamboo shoots can grow more than 30 centimetres in a single day, and may reach 30 metres in a single growing season. Slow-growing lichens may take 50 years to grow just one square centimetre!

SLOW GROWING
Lichen – 7 millimetres
per year

► Reindeer lichen can reach 100 years of age. When conditions are harsh it can stop growing completely and wait for warmer weather to return.

8 All plants are able to make new plants by a process called reproduction. Many plants grow flowers, which contain reproductive organs where seeds develop. Some flowers produce one seed, others produce millions.

9 People used to think that fungi, such as mushrooms, were plants. Now, scientists know they belong to a different group of living things. Fungi have some similarities to plants, but they lack the ability to make their own food.

▼ The most well-known fungi – mushrooms and toadstools – can be identified by their size, shape and colour.

Fairy ring mushroom

Field mushroom

Parasol

Devil's boletus

Fly agaric

Wood blewit

Many-zoned bracket fungus

Dryad's saddle

Death cap

Mealy tubaria

The family tree

10 If you could go back in time several million years you would see many plants different from those alive today. Plants change, or adapt, to suit changes in their habitat (natural home), and the ones that survive best are able to reproduce. This process is called evolution.

▶ Living things can be put into groups called kingdoms depending on their characteristics. Here, the Plant Kingdom is explained.

FUNGI KINGDOM

ANIMAL KINGDOM

Mosses

Mostly small, simple plants without tubes that transport water and food around.

PLANT KINGDOM

EARLY LIFE

11 The first plants probably lived in oceans, and were closely related to simple plants called algae (say: al-gee). Plants that existed long ago have lots in common with plants that evolved more recently. For example, all plants have a tough material called cellulose in their cell walls.

Green algae

Red algae

Brown algae

I DON'T BELIEVE IT!
Big plant-eating dinosaurs needed lots of food to survive. They trampled trees, and probably stripped entire forests clean.

ALGAE
Algae are similar to plants because they use the Sun's energy to make food. However, they do not have roots, leaves or stems. We call them seaweeds, and there are three main groups of algae: green, red and brown.

12 Mosses and liverworts are simple plants that grow in damp, shady places. They rarely grow more than a few centimetres tall, but gain height by growing on other plants. They do not have flowers, but reproduce using special cells called spores.

Liverworts

13 The first trees existed long before the dinosaurs and were similar to today's large ferns. Some ferns are only a few centimetres high, but the tallest grow into 20-metre-tall trees. Like mosses and liverworts, ferns reproduce by spores, which grow on the underside of each frond (leaf).

Seedless plants that reproduce by means of spores.

Ferns

Plants with tubes that transport food and water around. They can grow larger and are more complex.

Seed-producing plants that have reproductive parts. Seeds develop after fertilization (when a male cell and a female cell join together).

Conifers

14 Plants evolved seeds around 390 million years ago. These structures contain food reserves, which help new plants to grow. Early seed plants gave rise to a group called gymnosperms. Conifers, such as the huge giant sequoia, are gymnosperms.

15 Flowering plants, known as angiosperms, evolved at least 130 million years ago. At this time dinosaurs roamed the land and winged insects had existed for more than 175 million years. Humans evolved two million years ago.

Flowering plants

Sun-catchers

16 **Plants flourish all over the planet.** They can even be found in places where no animal can survive. This success is thanks to plants' special ability to photosynthesize – make their own food using sunlight.

▶ Leaves are green because of a green substance in their cells called chlorophyll that helps them to make food. Under a microscope, a leaf's different cells and tissues can be identified.

Leaf cross-section

Epidermis (outer layer)

Photosynthesis takes place in block-shaped palisade cells

Spongy cell layer

Bundles of tiny tubes transport substances around the plant

17 **Photosynthesis happens in leaves and it is one of nature's most incredible processes.** Plants use the energy from sunlight to turn carbon dioxide and water into sugar for food. Excess sugar is turned into a substance called starch, which is stored as reserve food supplies.

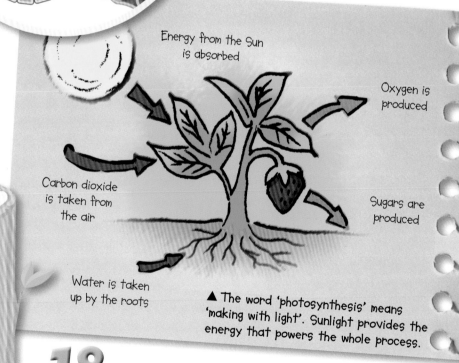

Energy from the Sun is absorbed

Oxygen is produced

Carbon dioxide is taken from the air

Sugars are produced

Water is taken up by the roots

▲ The word 'photosynthesis' means 'making with light'. Sunlight provides the energy that powers the whole process.

LIGHT AND DARK

You will need:
piece of card   scissors   paper clip

Cut a circle in the card and place it on the leaf of a living plant. Secure with the paper clip. After a few days, remove the card. The covered area will have faded. Why do you think this is?

Day one   Day four

18 **Plants need water, light, chlorophyll and carbon dioxide to photosynthesize.** Carbon dioxide gas, which is in air, enters the plant through tiny holes mainly on the underside of a leaf. During photosynthesis, oxygen – the gas that all animals breathe – is released as a waste product.

Round

Needle

Oval

Long

Compound

Pinnate

◀ Special words are used to describe leaf shapes. The largest leaves usually grow on trees that live in wet regions.

19 Leaves are sun-catchers. Most leaves are flat and broad so they can catch lots of light. Plants that grow in cold, windswept places and receive less sunlight have tough, needle-shaped leaves. They lose less water, which helps them to photosynthesize in winter.

▼ Beetles chomp their way through leaves, and can quickly strip plants bare.

20 Plants have stems that raise their leaves up towards the light. They have roots that grow below the ground and absorb water (see page 12). From its roots, water travels up through a plant's stem and into its leaves through tubes called xylem tubes.

21 The sugary food that plants make is the fuel that many of the world's animals depend on. Some animals eat plants, and this gives them energy. Those animals may be eaten by other animals, and so the Sun's energy is passed along the food chain.

Going underground

22 One of the most amazing parts of a plant — the roots — usually lies hidden from view, underground. Roots look like white sprawling threads and they have four important jobs to do for the plant.

23 Roots take up water from soil for use in photosynthesis. They also absorb minerals that are essential for the plant's growth. Roots help to anchor a plant in the soil and stop the soil blowing away, and they store food for the plant.

◄ In Mexico, the roots from a tree growing above ground have reached through a natural sinkhole to find water below.

▼ Most roots are long, white and slender, but they can grow in different ways, and in different forms.

Tuberous
Parts of the roots swell with stores of food

Adventitious
These roots are unusual because they grow down from the stems, branches or leaves of a plant

Fibrous
Many branching roots grow as a thick clump

Taproot
One main, thick root grows vertically downwards

24 Roots grow many smaller side roots and these are covered in millions of tiny 'hairs' that are excellent at absorbing water. A scientist studied one rye plant (a type of grass) and discovered that if all its 13 million side roots were laid end to end they would stretch for 500 kilometres!

▼ Waves and currents push and pull mangrove trees, but their prop roots help them to stay upright.

25 Some roots grow above and below the ground. These are called prop roots and they give a plant extra strength to grow tall and sturdy. Mangrove prop roots trap mud, helping to support the trees and protect coastal areas from storms.

26 Some orchids grow on rainforest trees, a long way above the soil. They have fleshy green roots that grow along branches or dangle downwards. These are called aerial roots.

Aerial roots

▲ An orchid's aerial roots absorb water straight from the air.

TRUE OR FALSE?

1. Roots grow towards light.
2. Mangrove trees have prop roots.
3. Roots can be good to eat.

Answers:
1. False 2. True 3. True

27 Some plants store water and energy as starch in their roots – and we use these roots as food. Carrots, beetroots and sweet potatoes are all formed from roots, or parts of roots, and grow underground. They are packed full of fibre and vitamins – both essential parts of a healthy diet.

Blooming marvellous

28 Flowers are often spectacular blooms that are colourful and perfumed to entice animals to come to them. They put on a showy display not to please our senses, but in a fierce bid to survive and reproduce.

Petal

The ovary contains ovules (female sex cells)

Sepals

▲ When a flower is cut in half, its sex organs can be seen. The ovary is normally hidden from view.

29 The petals of a flower surround a plant's sex organs. These parts produce and protect sex cells, which must come together before seeds can develop. A flower stays closed until the sex organs are fully mature, then the petals unfurl to attract insects and other animals to pollinate them (see page 16).

30 Bright yellow grains of pollen contain male sex cells. Pollen is produced on anthers, which are attached to stalks called filaments. Female sex cells are called ovules and they are produced in the flower's ovary.

◀ Vibrant pink petals help insects to find pollen at the centres of these cosmos flowers.

I DON'T BELIEVE IT!

Sweet-smelling rose petals are used to make perfume, skin creams and bath oils. In ancient Rome, women used to wash in baths full of rose petals!

Filament

Anthers contain
pollen grains
(male sex cells)

Stigma

31 Delicious smells and colourful petals help bring insects, or other animals, to a flower. Some petals have patterns that help to guide insects towards the flower's centre. As well as pollen, there is often a sweet liquid called nectar there.

In UV light

In natural light

◄▲ In ultraviolet light a silverweed flower appears as a bee would see it. The red shading is called a nectar guide — it guides the bee to pollen at the centre and a reward of nectar.

32 During their long history on Earth, flowering plants have evolved in many different ways to help reproduction. Some flowers are as big as dustbin lids, others are smaller than a pea. Some flowers stink of rotting flesh, while others resemble bees, slippers, bells or even trumpets!

► Flowers grow in many different colours, shapes and sizes to attract insects and other pollinating animals.

BUILT-IN PERCH

The bird of paradise flower provides a handy perch for its bird pollinators

IMITATION

An orchid looks like a female bee to attract male bees carrying pollen from other flowers

FOUL SMELL

The titan arum flower smells of rotting meat to attract flies

Perfect pollination

33 Bees, flies, butterflies and beetles perform a very important job – pollination. Many plants rely on insects to carry pollen from one flower to another, and they trick the insects into doing it.

34 Pollen grains are tiny so they are easily carried by insects. When a bug investigates inside a flower, anthers full of pollen rub against its body. Some pollen grains have tiny spines or hooks to catch onto the bodies of insects.

▼ Bees are some of the planet's most important pollinators because they visit many different plants.

Pollen sac

Anthers

◄ Under a powerful microscope pollen grains can be seen trapped in the thick coating of hairs on a bee's leg.

► The blue-tailed day lizard is the only known pollinator of the *Roussea simplex* flower of Mauritius.

35 Insects are not the only pollinators – bats, birds and lizards also help out. About 70 types of lizard visit flowers to feed on nectar and pollen. Some species of the Australian Banksia plant, recognized by their large flower spikes, produce more nectar at night to attract bats.

36 Not all flowers bother with fine looks and sweet smells to attract pollinators. Grasses don't rely on insects to carry their pollen, they let the wind do the job. These plants often have small flowers without petals or scent.

▲ A cloud of cocksfoot grass pollen is carried on the wind.

PARTS OF A FLOWER

Pollen grains on the stigma

Stigma

Style

Ovary

A pollen grain (male) joins with an ovule (female)

Pollen tube

▶ When a pollen grain lands on the stigma of a plant of the same species, it grows a tube down to the ovary.

37 When a pollen grain lands on a flower's stigma, pollination has taken place. The grain contains the male sex cell, which will fertilize an ovule (female sex cell). Only a fertilized ovule can grow into a seed.

Flower

Proboscis

Spur

38 Many animals have evolved alongside flowering plants, and they depend on each other to survive. Without pollination, most plants could not reproduce, and this would mean a shortage of food for land animals.

▶ The Morgan's Sphinx hawk moth is the only animal able to feed from the long spurs (tubes that contain nectar) of the comet orchid.

▶ Here, the moth's 25-centimetre-long proboscis (sucking mouthpart) is rolled up.

Travelling far

39 Plants are able to travel great distances, sometimes across entire oceans. That may come as a surprise because most plants are firmly rooted to the spot. However, when they are still seeds, some species make incredible journeys as they begin new lives.

▼ Protected by its buoyant waterproof outer case, a coconut can travel across an ocean to germinate on a new shore.

CANDELABRA LILY
NATIVE TO AFRICA

The spherical seed heads dry and then snap off. They are rolled along by the wind, scattering seeds as they travel.

HIMALAYAN BALSAM
NATIVE TO THE HIMALAYAS

The 8-millimetre-long seed pods explode when touched, propelling seeds up to 7 metres away.

▶ Seeds can be spread by a variety of methods, including by wind or animals.

40 Plants want their seeds to grow far away from them. That way, the seedlings will not fight with their parent plants for light, water and space. So plants have developed ingenious ways to send their offspring far away.

I DON'T BELIEVE IT!

Squirting cucumbers can shoot their seeds 5 metres away. Their seedpods are full of water and explode at the slightest touch.

MILKWEED
NATIVE TO NORTH AMERICA

The lightweight seeds have tufts of silky hair and are carried by the wind, travelling like tiny parachutes.

41 Some plants have shaped seed cases that help seeds 'fly' through the air. They act like parachutes, helicopters or gliders, carrying their seeds to new places. Some seed cases explode, propelling their seeds through the air and away from the parent plant.

42 Fruit seeds are often wrapped in sweet, juicy flesh to tempt animals to eat them. The seeds are tough enough to pass through the animals' bodies unharmed and come out in droppings. The droppings contain nutrients, which help the seeds to grow into plants.

Close-up of burdock hooks

◀▼ It's easy to see why burdock seed cases were the inspiration behind the invention of Velcro, the hook-and--loop fastening system.

Bur in wool

43 Seeds with prickles, called burs, can hitch a lift on animals. Tiny hooks on burdock seed cases become attached to the fur of animals as they pass by. Eventually, some burs fall out of the animals' fur and may grow into new plants in new places.

Starting again

44 When a seed comes to rest in a suitable place with suitable conditions, it starts to grow. This is called germination and it marks the beginning of a new plant's life. All seeds need water and oxygen to germinate, and some need warmth too.

▼ Each sorus (spore-producing spot) on a fern can release thousands of tiny spores when ripe.

45 The first part of a plant to grow from the seed during germination is a special root called a radicle. A stem grows next, with leaf-like structures called cotyledons. Then tiny leaves appear and an adult plant develops.

▼ A seed needs the right conditions to germinate.

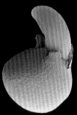

③ The radicle begins to grow downwards

① The radicle tip breaks through the seed casing

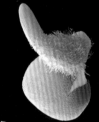

② Root hairs develop on the radicle

④ The leaf-like cotyledons grow upwards

▶ Despite the barren-looking landscape, a coconut has germinated in a lava field. Its fibrous roots can be seen

46 Mosses, liverworts, ferns and fungi don't have seeds, but produce tiny cells called spores instead. Spores grow on the underside of a fern's leaves, inside round 'spots' called sori. When the spores are released, they are carried on the wind.

47 Huge numbers of acacia tree seed pods are devoured by African elephants. Acacia seeds travel through an elephant's digestive system and are excreted in waste called dung. Many of the acacia seeds germinate, and grow into trees in new places.

◀▲ Most of the acacia seeds in this dung will germinate because they are in a warm, wet and nutritious fertilizer.

Spring

Winter

▲▶ Bluebells flower in spring. Then they die down and survive the winter as bulbs underground, until the following spring.

48 Starting again doesn't always mean growing from seed. Some plants, such as strawberries, produce 'baby' plants on long stems called runners. New potato plants can grow from 'eyes' – small spots on the potato's skin where shoots grow. Pieces of stems or leaves may also grow into new plants.

49 When plants disappear over winter, they do not always die. Many survive just as roots, or as special structures called bulbs. The new shoots that grow in spring sprout from dormant roots or bulbs, which have stored food ready for the plant to grow again when the conditions are right.

SOWING SEEDS

You will need:
saucer   cotton wool
mustard and cress seeds

1. Put some cotton wool on a saucer and moisten it.
2. Sprinkle mustard and cress seeds on top of the damp cotton wool and leave in a warm, sunny spot.
3. Within a day, the seeds will begin to germinate.

Snaps, traps and sticky bits

50 In places where there is little light or few nutrients in the soil, some plants have developed extraordinary ways to feed. Although these plants can still photosynthesize, they break the rules because they also get energy from 'eating' insects and small organisms. These are the green, mean meat-eaters!

① A fly touches sensitive trigger hairs as it crawls along the trap

51 The Venus flytrap is the most famous of all meat-eating plants. Equipped with touch-sensitive trigger hairs, the flytrap's leaves sense when a bug crawls inside, and snap shut. Strong juices called enzymes are then poured over the bug so it can be digested (broken down).

▶ Venus flytraps grow naturally in bogs and other wet habitats in the United States.

52 Pitcher plants catch prey using sweet-smelling, slippery-sided deathtraps. Pitchers look like upturned trumpets, and they hold pools of water in their bases. Insects are attracted by perfume and nectar, but when they land they slip down the trumpet's waxy sides and drown in the pool. Strong acids hasten their death.

◀ A fly cannot clamber out of a pitcher plant, because of its slippery sides.

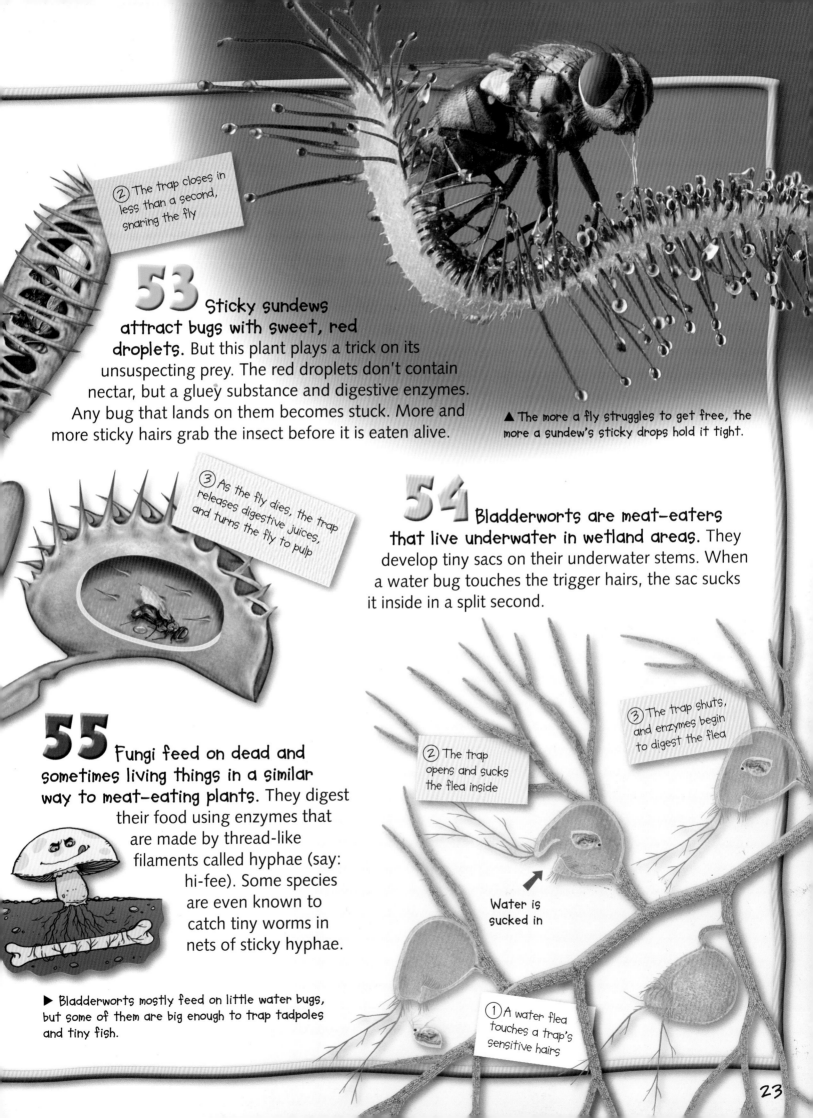

② The trap closes in less than a second, sharing the fly

53 Sticky sundews attract bugs with sweet, red droplets. But this plant plays a trick on its unsuspecting prey. The red droplets don't contain nectar, but a gluey substance and digestive enzymes. Any bug that lands on them becomes stuck. More and more sticky hairs grab the insect before it is eaten alive.

▲ The more a fly struggles to get free, the more a sundew's sticky drops hold it tight.

③ As the fly dies, the trap releases digestive juices, and turns the fly to pulp

54 Bladderworts are meat-eaters that live underwater in wetland areas. They develop tiny sacs on their underwater stems. When a water bug touches the trigger hairs, the sac sucks it inside in a split second.

55 Fungi feed on dead and sometimes living things in a similar way to meat-eating plants. They digest their food using enzymes that are made by thread-like filaments called hyphae (say: hi-fee). Some species are even known to catch tiny worms in nets of sticky hyphae.

▶ Bladderworts mostly feed on little water bugs, but some of them are big enough to trap tadpoles and tiny fish.

③ The trap shuts, and enzymes begin to digest the flea

② The trap opens and sucks the flea inside

Water is sucked in

① A water flea touches a trap's sensitive hairs

Friends and enemies

56 Plants and animals depend upon one another. But the relationship is not always one of co-operation – it's a battle for survival. Sometimes the best way to survive is to get along, but at other times, the fight is on!

57 Arolla pine trees grow in high mountains thanks to alpine nutcrackers. These birds gather the seeds and hide them in the ground as food stores. Some seeds germinate and new forests grow.

▶ In the South American rainforest, sloths are camouflaged well thanks to the green algae that grows in their fur. Sloths also play host to moths, which feed on the green algae and lay eggs in the sloths' dung.

Moth in fur

58 Some ants make nests in the thorns of acacia trees, but the trees tolerate this invasion. The ants defend the tree by stinging browsing animals and cutting through tendrils of nearby plants. In return, the tree rewards the ants with food packets that grow on its leaflet tips.

▼ Ants work hard to defend their acacia home.

Ants bite browsing animals

Ant nest inside a hollow thorn

Nectar glands provide ants with a sweet drink

59 There is fierce competition for light in dense tropical forests. Strangler figs wrap their roots and stems around trees and, over many years, eventually kill them. The strangler fig's roots take all the water from the soil, and its leaves block light from the host tree.

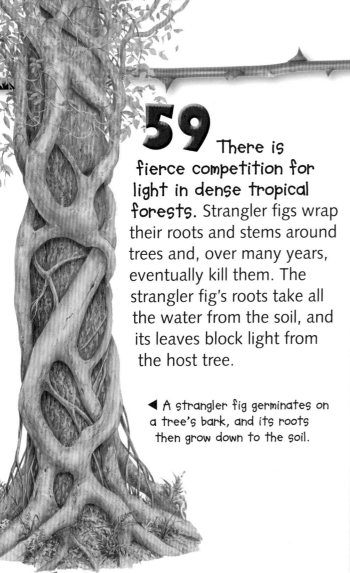

◄ A strangler fig germinates on a tree's bark, and its roots then grow down to the soil.

60 Plants have several ways to defend themselves against animals. Spines, stinging hairs, thorns and foul-tasting parts are good ways to deter animals from eating leaves or flowers. Unripe fruit often tastes bad to prevent animals from eating it before the seeds inside are ready.

► Plants need to attract animals for pollination, but too much damage by plant-eaters can be harmful, so defences are essential.

Ants gather nutritious food packets and take them back to the nest

▼ Goats don't mind climbing spiny Argan trees to reach the leaves and fruit, but this can cause a lot of damage.

PLANT DEFENCES

Horse chestnuts have tough, prickly seed cases.

Stinging nettles have sharp hairs that inject a burning chemical.

Roses have thorns that catch and tear skin.

Unripe persimmon fruits taste too bitter for most animals.

Ragwort's yellow flowers are poisonous to horses and other animals.

Thrive and survive

61 Plants are able to adapt. They can live on cliff faces, and inside giant clams in the sea. They can even survive under metres of snow, in rivers or beneath the hot desert Sun. Plants have evolved to exist in almost every habitat on Earth.

▼ The fat stems of a cactus store water when it rains for use in dry times.

▼ The flowers of the Arctic poppy move to follow the Sun across the sky, which makes them warmer and more attractive to pollinating insects.

62 Many desert-living plants can store water – a handy adaption in hot, dry environments. A giant saguaro cactus may hold several tonnes of water in its stems. Quiver trees can lose whole branches to save water when conditions get too dry.

63 Summer at the Earth's polar regions may last no more than a few days, and there is little warmth or sunshine through the year. Even water is a problem because it is locked up as ice. Despite this, plants survive – tiny algae have been found living inside rocks.

QUIZ

1. What spiny plants live in deserts?
2. How do cushion plants stay out of the wind?
3. What habitat is home to many grazing animals?

Answers:
1. Cacti 2. They grow low to the ground 3. Grasslands or plains

64 Fierce winds and cold air make life tough for plants living on mountains or high plains. Plants that survive are mainly low-growing and some form dense mats. These are called cushion plants, and scientists have found the temperature in their centres to be a few degrees higher than the surrounding air.

▼ A cushion plant survives cold winds by growing close to the ground. Its dense green surface absorbs and traps lots of heat from the Sun.

▼ The enormous prairies of North America cover 3 million square kilometres. Many animals, including bison, graze on them.

65 Grass often grows on huge plains where there is too little rain for trees to survive. In North America these are called prairies and they are home to many types of grazers – animals that feed on grass. Shoots of grass grow from the ground, and keep growing after the tops have been eaten. Grasses also have complex root systems that spread out in wide networks to absorb water.

66 When scientists discovered some 2000–year–old magnolia seeds they decided to try and grow one – and succeeded! When conditions are difficult, plants can survive as seeds. These small packages contain all the information a plant needs to germinate and grow when the time is right.

Life underwater

67 Plants that live in ponds, rivers and seas have plenty of nutrients and water – but lack of light can be a problem. Light doesn't travel through water as easily as it does through air. Giant water lilies combat this problem by growing enormous sun-catching leaves.

◀ Long stalks raise the water lily's leaves and flowers to the surface.

68 Water lilies keep their leaves above water, but some flowering plants live most of their lives entirely submerged. Their leaves are able to absorb gases from the water, so they can still photosynthesize. However, flowers must still poke above the water so insects or the wind can pollinate them.

69 Algae, including seaweed, are not true plants but are similar in that they share the extraordinary ability to photosynthesize. Some algae consist of a single cell and are only visible under a microscope. Others are huge – fronds of giant kelp can reach 45 metres in length.

▶ A raft of kelp drifting in the sea provides shelter for small fish, making it difficult for predators to catch them.

70 Beautiful coral reefs are home to billions of sea creatures, but they would not exist without the help of tiny algae. These algae live inside the bodies of coral polyps, which build the reef. The polyps provide a safe home for the algae, and the algae supply the polyps with food and the oxygen they need to breathe.

71 There are about 10,000 species of seaweed in the world. Most of them are red, but there are brown and green types too. Seaweeds have holdfasts, rather than roots, which enable them to stick firmly to rocks even when waves thrash them around.

▼ There are thousands of different types of algae, and many of them are seaweeds.

SEAWEED TYPES

Bladderwrack

Dulse

Knotted Wrack

Sea Lettuce

Oarweed

Kelp

▼ In the right conditions, microscopic algae can suddenly grow into huge groups called blooms.

72 Microscopic green algae in the oceans play an important part in supporting life on Earth. There are billions and billions of them, and they are food for many animals. They also produce much of the oxygen that goes into our atmosphere.

Forests of the world

73 Trees are long-living plants with stems that become thick and woody with age. A trunk can support heavy branches and thousands of leaves. Many trees growing in one place create a forest.

▼ As a tree grows it produces more layers of cells, or rings, in its trunk. These can provide clues about past climates.

Fast growth in warm or rainy season

First year growth

Slow growth in dry or cold season

Scar from forest fire

74 A forest is an ecosystem. This is a place where animals and plants live together, and depend on each other. A single tree provides a home for many animals, from the dead leaves around its base, to its branch tips. Some bugs and fungi live beneath a tree's bark.

KEY
1 Badger
2 Beetle
3 Worm
4 Mole
5 Hedgehog
6 Fox
7 Butterfly
8 Squirrel
9 Chipmunk
10 Tawny owl
11 Jay

▶ Deciduous forests grow throughout Europe and in eastern USA. They provide a range of habitats for a huge diversity of wildlife.

DECIDUOUS FOREST

CANOPY

UNDERSTOREY

GROUND LEVEL

75 Forests can grow wherever there is enough warmth and water for trees to live. There are different types of forest, and each type requires different climatic conditions (temperature, winds and rainfall) to grow.

76 Temperate forests grow in mild climates. Types of temperate forest include deciduous, where trees lose their leaves in autumn in preparation for winter, and temperate rainforest, where there is high rainfall.

▲ Unlike tropical rainforests, temperate rainforests have seasons and less variety of plant species. This type of forest can be found in western USA.

77 Coniferous forests generally grow in cool places, often close to the Arctic region. The trees here are conifers, which have thin, needle-like leaves, and reproduce using cones. They are adapted for life in harsh conditions of snow, frost and wind.

▼ Tropical rainforests grow in a narrow zone north and south of the Equator (an imaginary line around the centre of the Earth). They receive rain and heat all year round.

CONIFEROUS FOREST

▲ Coniferous forests grow where there are cold winters and warm summers.

QUIZ

1. What type of forest grows near the Equator?
2. What type of trees grow cones?
3. Where do worms live – in leaf litter or a forest canopy?

Answers:
1. Tropical rainforest
2. Conifers 3. Leaf litter

TROPICAL RAINFOREST

Lush jungles

78 Rainforests grow in places where there is at least 180 centimetres of rain each year. There needs to be rain most days, not just at certain seasons. Generally, rainforests grow in the warm region of the world known as the tropics, near the Equator.

RAINFOREST LAYERS

Emergent layer

Canopy

Understorey

Forest floor

▲ Scientists divide a rainforest and its plants into layers. Each layer provides a habitat for different animals.

Orchid

Passionflower

Heliconia

▲ An orang-utan feasts on the fruit of a tree in the rainforest in Borneo.

◀ Rainforest flowers are often described as exotic. They have vivid colours and unusual shapes.

79 Tropical rainforests are lush, green places that benefit from both heavy rainfall and heat all year round. They are sometimes called jungles. Without seasons, plants grow all year round, which means there is an endless supply of flowers and fruit for animals to eat.

Vanilla
orchid

Coffee
berries

Banana
palm flower

Cocoa
pods

Rubber
tree

Vanilla
pods

Coffee beans

Bananas

Chocolate

Rubber
tyre

◀ Rainforest
plants such as
bananas have been
grown in large quantities as
crops, and their products are
sold around the world.

80 Cloud forests
grow high in hills and near
mountaintops. The air in these
rainforests is especially damp, and
mist and low-level cloud cover the
treetops. There are cloud forests in
South America, Indonesia and parts
of Africa, where mountain gorillas
live in these damp habitats.

82 Many natural materials and foods come
from the rainforest. Rubber, chocolate, bananas,
coffee, vanilla, cinnamon and chicle (which is used to
make chewing gum) all come from plants that grow in
tropical forests. Precious woods, such as mahogany
and ebony, also grow there.

81 Rainforests provide food
and shelter for many people.
Families of the Korowai and
Kombai tribes of Papua
New Guinea live in
treehouses to stay safe
from attack by other
tribes. They find
everything they need
in the forest, and
hunt, fish and collect
plants to eat.

▶ The air is thick
and damp with mist in
a Costa Rican cloud
forest. Water drips from
leaves and steam rises
from the ground.

All around us

83 Plants are all around us — not just in our fields and gardens, but in our homes too. We breathe the oxygen they make, we eat them, we build with them and we enjoy watching them grow.

▲ Central Park in the middle of the city of New York, USA, covers more than 3 square kilometres.

Fruit and vegetables

Cereal, potatoes, pulses and bread

Sugars and fats

Meat, eggs and dairy products

84 From bulbs and tubers to leaves and beans, the energy, fibre and vitamins in plants keep our bodies healthy. Wheat, soya, corn and rice are staples — they provide most of the energy we need.

◄ The portions of what foods make up a healthy diet. Plants, and foods made from them, make up most of it.

▼ As well as food, materials such as cotton come from plants. Cotton has been used by humans for over 5000 years.

Cotton plant

85 Growing plants for our own use is called agriculture, and humans have been doing it for 10–15,000 years. The first plants people grew probably included barley, and beans. With advances in technology and farming methods, farms today produce a wide variety of crops.

86 Beautiful flowers are used to decorate homes, people, and even animals in some cultures. They play an important part in many festivals and ceremonies. Growing flowers for sale is called floriculture, and people who sell flowers are florists.

▼ The Netherlands is known for its huge flower farms where beautiful blooms — especially tulips — are grown.

87 Coal is a solid fuel that helped the modern world to develop steam power, factories and transport systems. It was formed millions of years ago, when ancient forests died and turned into a black rock that is packed with energy.

88 For thousands of years people have used plants to treat diseases. Now scientists are discovering ways that plants can help us to develop better medicines. They also know that some plants harm us: tobacco, which is in cigarettes, comes from the leaves of tobacco plants and causes lung and heart diseases.

Pomegranate
Scientists think this fruit may help fight cancer

Mint
This herb is traditionally used to treat stomach problems and pains

Echinacea
This flower is used to treat colds

Willow bark
This was used to develop aspirin, which treats pain

Ginseng
Some people believe this plant gives them more energy

▶ Plants are still used in many medicines and treatments today.

Plants in peril

89 When plants photosynthesize they produce oxygen – the gas that all animals need to breathe. Plants also absorb carbon dioxide. This changes the climate since extra carbon dioxide in the atmosphere makes our planet warmer.

90 When large areas of plants are destroyed, the way that energy, water and gases move through the world's systems is affected. The removal of many trees is called deforestation. This process releases carbon dioxide into the air, ruins the soil and can even change local weather systems.

▼ Rainforests in Borneo are being cut down at an alarming rate. Orang-utans, which live in these rainforests, will soon be homeless.

91 In some countries people have to cut down trees for fuel. Without the money to buy other kinds of fuel, they build fires for cooking, boiling water and to keep their families warm. It is also common for natural habitats to be turned into farmland, or grazing areas for animals.

I DON'T BELIEVE IT!

Nearly half of all the trees that are cut down are used to make paper – more than 300 million tonnes every year.

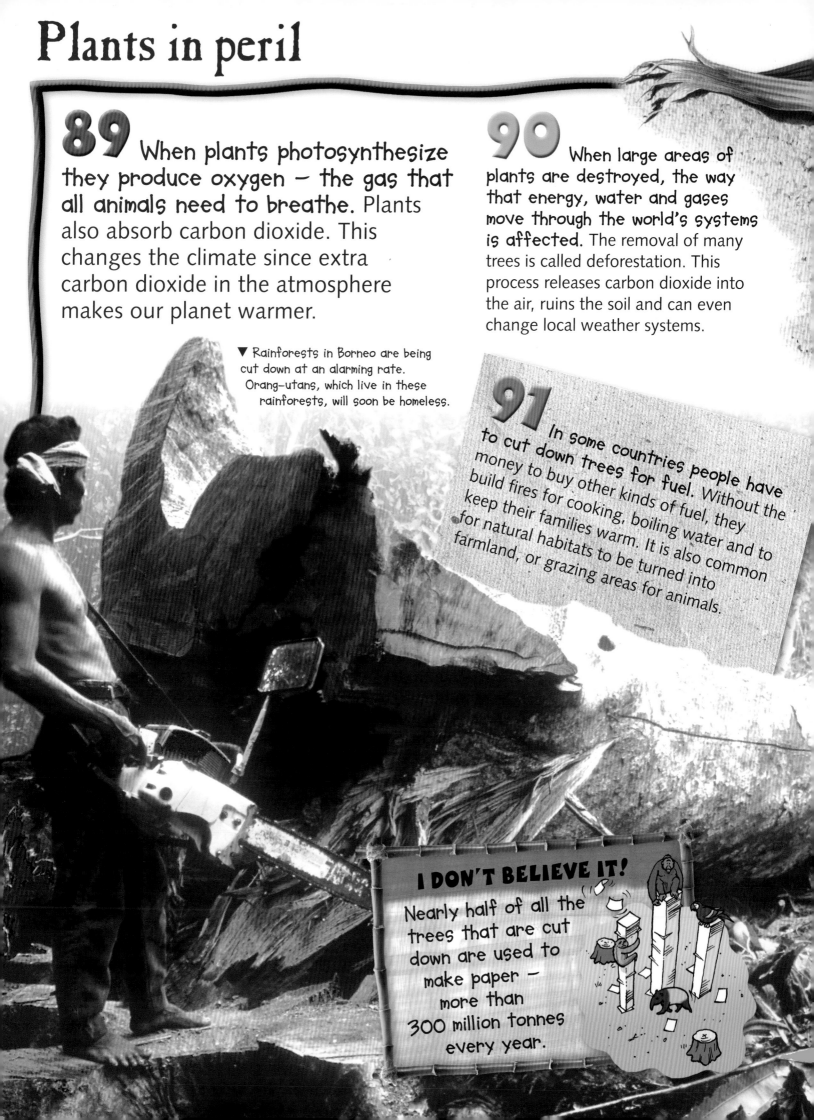

92 When plants are removed from an ecosystem there are no roots to hold the soil in place. Wind and rain sweep the soil away, leaving bare rocks or sand as a desert develops. Very few types of plant can survive in these new desert areas.

◀ The welwitschia is one of the few plants that survive in the deserts of Africa, even when there is no rain for months.

▼ The devastating effects of acid rain can turn a green forest into a dry, barren land.

93 The survival of some plants is threatened by acid rain. This is caused by pollution, such as carbon dioxide in the air, which changes rain water and makes it harmful. It pollutes lakes and ponds, poisoning fish and other animals, and it can kill trees.

▼ Scientists closely monitor how pollution in the air and in the soil affect the way that plants grow.

94 Scientists believe that one in five types of plants is in danger of becoming extinct – dying out forever. Humans are mostly to blame for this because we cut down trees and remove natural habitats to farm or graze our animals on. The building of houses and roads in these areas increases pollution levels.

The future is green

95 Scientists are helping people to understand how precious plants are. If we care for our planet today, future generations will be able to enjoy it. We must use the planet's resources responsibly.

96 Some farmers who used wood for fuel now use other sources of energy. Solar lamps use energy from the Sun, and biogas from dung or rotting food is used to power ovens, lights and even machinery.

FUEL SHED

▶ Yosemite National Park is a reserve in the USA where ancient giant sequoia trees are protected.

97 Natural areas called nature reserves help to save threatened plant species because their habitats are protected. Tourists and scientists visit the reserves to learn about plants and their ecosystems, which brings in much-needed funds.

QUIZ
1. What is the champion tree-growing nation?
2. Where are seeds stored: seed banks or seed cellars?
3. Where does solar energy come from?

Answers:
1. China 2. Seed banks
3. The Sun

98
China is the champion tree-growing nation. Many nations hope to halt deforestation. With China leading the way, ten percent more trees are expected in the world by 2050 – enough to cover an area the size of India.

▶ More than 25,000 new trees were planted during this reforestation project in Haiti, in 2010.

◀ Seeds are carefully labelled and kept safe in this seed bank in Germany.

99
Saving seeds stops some plant species becoming extinct. Worldwide, scientists are collecting seeds from native plants, especially rare species, and storing them in seed banks. These huge seed collections are protected and studied to ensure that these plants are conserved for the future.

▼ The world's largest greenhouse is at the Eden Project in the UK. Many plants from around the world are grown here.

100
Plants are part of our everyday lives, and how we choose to live plays a part in the planet's future. Protecting and growing plants in our habitats – homes, parks, gardens and schools – is a great way to begin a lifetime's journey into the world of plants.

Index

Page numbers in **bold** refer to main entries, those in *italics* refer to illustrations